Jumping Spiders

Trace Taylor

Body Parts

See that spider with the eyes.

See that spider with the legs.

See that spider with the arms.

See that spider with the fangs.

See that spider with the hair.

See that spider with the berries.

See that spider with the flower.

See that spider with the stick.

Predator & Prey

See that spider with the caterpillar.

See that spider with the ant.

See that spider with the fly.

See that spider with the spider.

See that spider with the butterfly.

See that spider with the bird.

I can use the first letter sound to match the word to the picture.

stick

berries

flower

caterpillar